MW01055511

FOLLOWING A FAITH

A Christian life

Cath Senker

PowerKiDS press

Published in 2020 by **The Rosen Publishing Group, Inc.**
29 East 21st Street, New York, NY 10010

Cataloging-in-Publication Data

Names: Senker, Cath.
Title: A Christian life / Cath Senker.
Description: New York : PowerKids Press, 2020. | Series: Following a faith |
Includes glossary and index.
Identifiers: ISBN 9781725303454 (pbk.) | ISBN 9781725303478 (library bound) |
ISBN 9781725303461 (6pack)
Subjects: LCSH: Christianity--Juvenile literature. | Fasts and feasts--Juvenile literature.
Classification: LCC BR125.5 S46 2020 | DDC 230--dc23

Credits
Series Editor: Amy Pimperton/Julia Bird
Series Designer: Krina Patel

Picture credits:ABACA/PA Images: 15t. Billion Photos/Shutterstock: 12b. Victor Borg/
Alamy: 11. S.Borisov/Shutterstock: 26. Christian Aid: 23. Perry Correll/Shutterstock:
14t. Sebastian Czapnik/Dreamstime: 19t. Daseaford/Dreamstime: 20. Design Pics/
Superstock: 13b. Don Despain/Alamy: front cover main. digital imagination/
istockphoto: 27. Michael Dwyer/Alamy: 9b. fototaler/Shutterstock: 29b. Angelo
Giampiccolo/Shutterstock: 7t. gkuna/Shutterstock: 12 main. Mike Goldwater/Alamy:
10t. Paul Gordon /Alamy: 25b. Hiper Com/Shutterstock: 1, 17. Robert Huberman/
Superstock: 5t. Jorisvo/Dreamstime: 14b. Jorisvo/Shutterstock: 18. Jovanas/123RF:
front cover c. Jurij Krupiak/Shutterstock: 25t. Kzenon/Shutterstock: 29t. Paddy
McGuiness/Alamy: 6. Nagel Photography/Shutterstock: 5b. Photocell/Dreamstime:
16. Gino Rigucci/Dreamstime: 10b. Frances Roberts/Alamy: 22c. Helene Rogers/Ark
Religion/Alamy: 28. Rosebud Pictures/Getty Images: 7b. Sjors737/Dreamstime: 13t.
Jason Smalley Photography/Alamy: 22b. Friedrich Stark/Alamy: 19b. Rolland Stoliner/
Dreamstim; 21. Untitled/Shutterstock: 4. Dmitry Vereshchagin/Shutterstock: 15b.
Wedding Stock Photo/Shutterstock: 24. wideonet/Shutterstock: 9t. Andreas Zerndll/
Shutterstock: 8

The author and publishers would like to thank the following people or organizations
whose material is included in this book: The Reverend Charles Royden: p.18; Martin
Poole, St Luke's Church: p.23;

Manufactured in the United States of America

CPSIA Compliance Information: Batch CSPK19: For Further Information contact Rosen Publishing,
New York, New York at 1-800-237-9932.

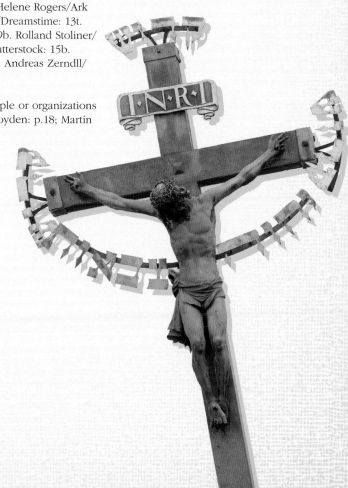

CONTENTS

WHAT DOES IT MEAN TO BE A CHRISTIAN?

If you are a Christian, you are one of a vast global community of more than two billion people. Christianity is the most common religion in the world. Find out what it is like to live as a Christian, the main rites of passage, and how Christians celebrate their festivals throughout the year.

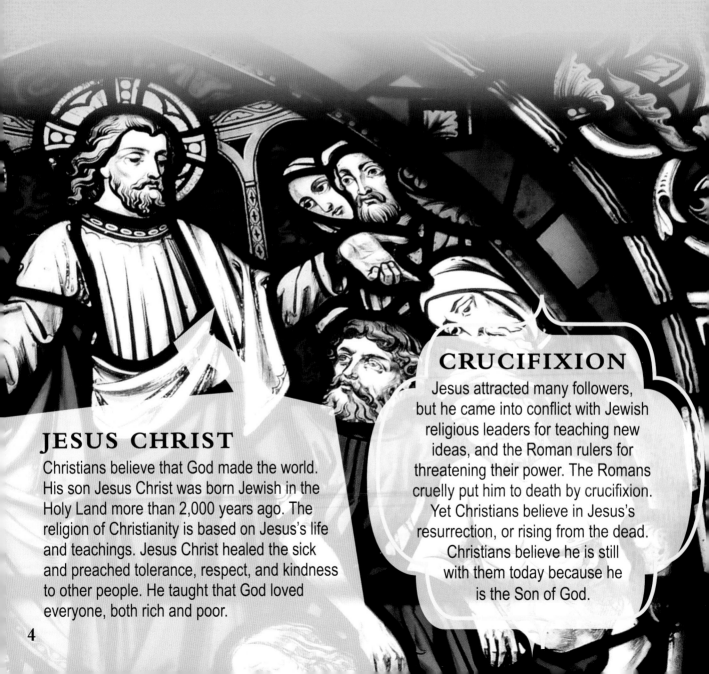

JESUS CHRIST

Christians believe that God made the world. His son Jesus Christ was born Jewish in the Holy Land more than 2,000 years ago. The religion of Christianity is based on Jesus's life and teachings. Jesus Christ healed the sick and preached tolerance, respect, and kindness to other people. He taught that God loved everyone, both rich and poor.

CRUCIFIXION

Jesus attracted many followers, but he came into conflict with Jewish religious leaders for teaching new ideas, and the Roman rulers for threatening their power. The Romans cruelly put him to death by crucifixion. Yet Christians believe in Jesus's resurrection, or rising from the dead. Christians believe he is still with them today because he is the Son of God.

THE HOLY BIBLE

The work and teachings of Jesus are written in a book called the Holy Bible. It also contains stories about the Jewish people and the first Christians. The Bible provides rules for living; the most important are the Ten Commandments. Christians also follow the example of saints – holy people who lived good lives and helped others.

Christians and Jews follow the Ten Commandments.

THE TEN COMMANDMENTS

To Christians, these commandments are a vital set of rules that God expects people to live by. The commandments tell them how to practice their faith and behave toward others. Christians should worship God and no other and keep Sunday as a special day for prayer. Respecting their mother and father is another rule. They should never kill anyone, steal, or tell lies.

BORN INTO CHRISTIANITY

Christian parents bring up their children in the faith from the very start. They welcome a new baby into the family with the ceremony of baptism. It is also called a christening because children are given their Christian names at this time. Normally, babies are baptized when they are just a few weeks or months old.

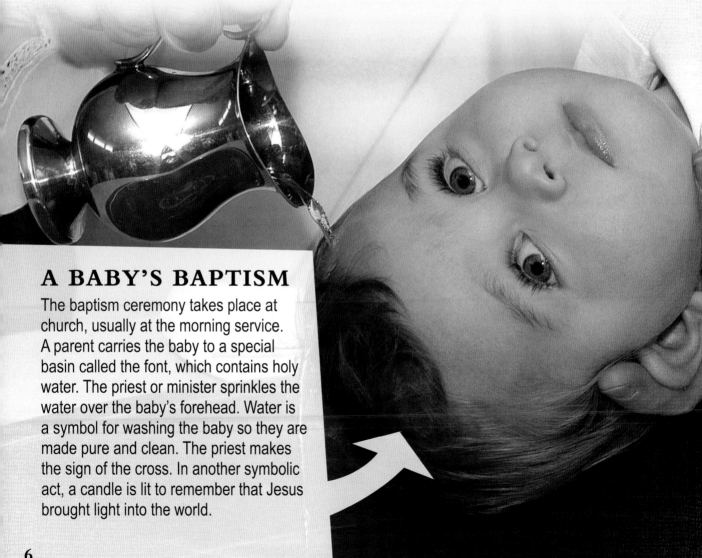

A BABY'S BAPTISM

The baptism ceremony takes place at church, usually at the morning service. A parent carries the baby to a special basin called the font, which contains holy water. The priest or minister sprinkles the water over the baby's forehead. Water is a symbol for washing the baby so they are made pure and clean. The priest makes the sign of the cross. In another symbolic act, a candle is lit to remember that Jesus brought light into the world.

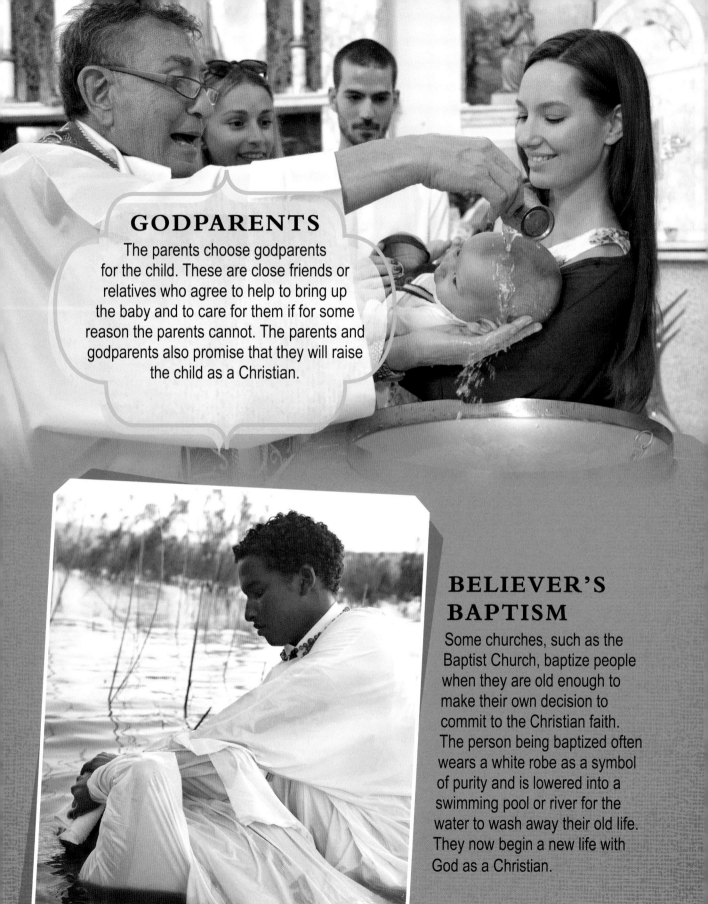

GODPARENTS

The parents choose godparents for the child. These are close friends or relatives who agree to help to bring up the baby and to care for them if for some reason the parents cannot. The parents and godparents also promise that they will raise the child as a Christian.

BELIEVER'S BAPTISM

Some churches, such as the Baptist Church, baptize people when they are old enough to make their own decision to commit to the Christian faith. The person being baptized often wears a white robe as a symbol of purity and is lowered into a swimming pool or river for the water to wash away their old life. They now begin a new life with God as a Christian.

GOING TO CHURCH

Many Christians go to church to strengthen their connection to God and their community. Churches come in all shapes and sizes, from magnificent cathedrals to tiny chapels.

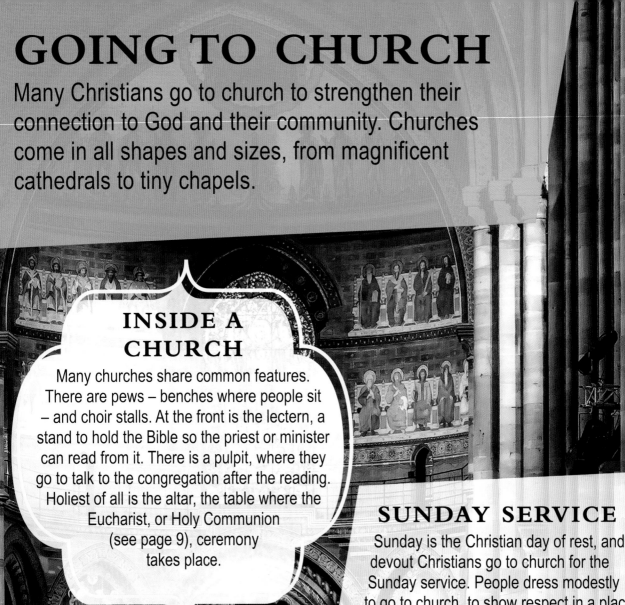

INSIDE A CHURCH

Many churches share common features. There are pews – benches where people sit – and choir stalls. At the front is the lectern, a stand to hold the Bible so the priest or minister can read from it. There is a pulpit, where they go to talk to the congregation after the reading. Holiest of all is the altar, the table where the Eucharist, or Holy Communion (see page 9), ceremony takes place.

SUNDAY SERVICE

Sunday is the Christian day of rest, and devout Christians go to church for the Sunday service. People dress modestly to go to church, to show respect in a place of worship. The priest or minister leads the service. In some churches, he or she wears ceremonial robes. At all church services, people pray to God, but the service varies greatly depending on the branch of the church. The atmosphere may be solemn, with people singing traditional hymns, or lively, with loud rock music. In some churches, gospel choirs sing rousing songs to praise God, and everyone joins in.

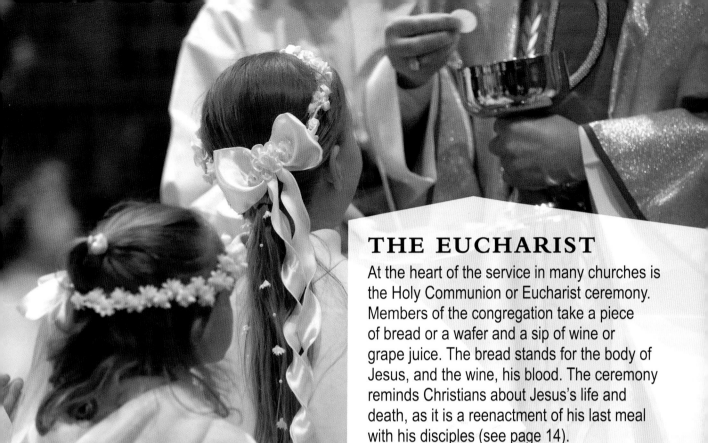

THE EUCHARIST

At the heart of the service in many churches is the Holy Communion or Eucharist ceremony. Members of the congregation take a piece of bread or a wafer and a sip of wine or grape juice. The bread stands for the body of Jesus, and the wine, his blood. The ceremony reminds Christians about Jesus's life and death, as it is a reenactment of his last meal with his disciples (see page 14).

SUNDAY SCHOOL

Before, during, or after the service, young children often attend Sunday school. They read Bible stories about Jesus's teachings and learn prayers. The children may explore their faith through enjoyable activities such as art, crafts, and music.

LIGHT

In many churches, people light a candle as a symbol of God's presence. It symbolizes prayer, too. For Christians, "being in the light" also means treating other people well.

CELEBRATING CHRISTMAS

As well as the weekly routine of going to church, Christians follow a calendar of religious events throughout the year. At Christmas, Christians celebrate a significant date in their history – the birth of Jesus on a cold, winter night in a stable in Bethlehem. Most Christians celebrate Jesus's birthday on December 25; some Orthodox Churches celebrate it on January 6 or January 7.

NATIVITY PLAYS

At school, children may act out the story of Jesus's birth. Jesus's parents, Joseph and Mary, had to go to Joseph's hometown, Bethlehem, for a census – a counting of the people. The local inn was full so the innkeeper let them stay overnight in the stable. It was there that the baby Jesus came into the world and was welcomed as the Son of God.

PREPARING AT HOME

Families often set up a nativity scene at home. They arrange models of Mary, Joseph, the baby Jesus, and the animals in the stable, with the three wise men bringing gifts for the newborn baby.

TREES

The tradition of putting up a tree dates to pre-Christian times. An evergreen tree was a symbol of new life in winter. From the Middle Ages (c. 500–1500), trees became a symbol of Christmas.

PRAYERS AND PRESENTS

On Christmas Eve, many Catholics go to a midnight mass service – even children stay up late to attend. They listen to the sermon, sing carols, take Holy Communion, and say prayers.

In many countries, Christmas Day is a holiday. Christians go to church. During the service, the priest reads the prophecy of Jesus's birth from the Book of Isaiah in the Bible: *"For to us a child is born, to us a son is given."* People sing joyful carols. Afterwards, they may go home for a big Christmas dinner. They may also exchange presents and cards, to remind them of God's gift of his son Jesus.

CHRISTMAS CAROLS

Most carols are less than 200 years old. "Silent Night," "Good King Wenceslas," and "O Little Town of Bethlehem" were all written in the 19th century.

11

LENT

The period of time that is known as Lent in the Christian calendar falls on the 40 days (not counting Sundays) before Easter. It is a time for Christians to reflect on their faith.

TIME TO THINK

During Lent, Christians remember when Jesus chose to spend forty days fasting and praying in the Judaean desert to prepare for his work for God. They recall how he suffered and later gave up his life to pay for people's sins. Christians think about what they have done wrong and ask God for forgiveness, and they consider how to be kinder to others.

SACRIFICE

During Lent, many Christians give up certain foods to strengthen their faith. Some may even fast, or not eat, some of the time. Orthodox Christians stop eating meat and dairy products. Western Christians usually give up a food they love – often a luxury such as chocolate or cake.

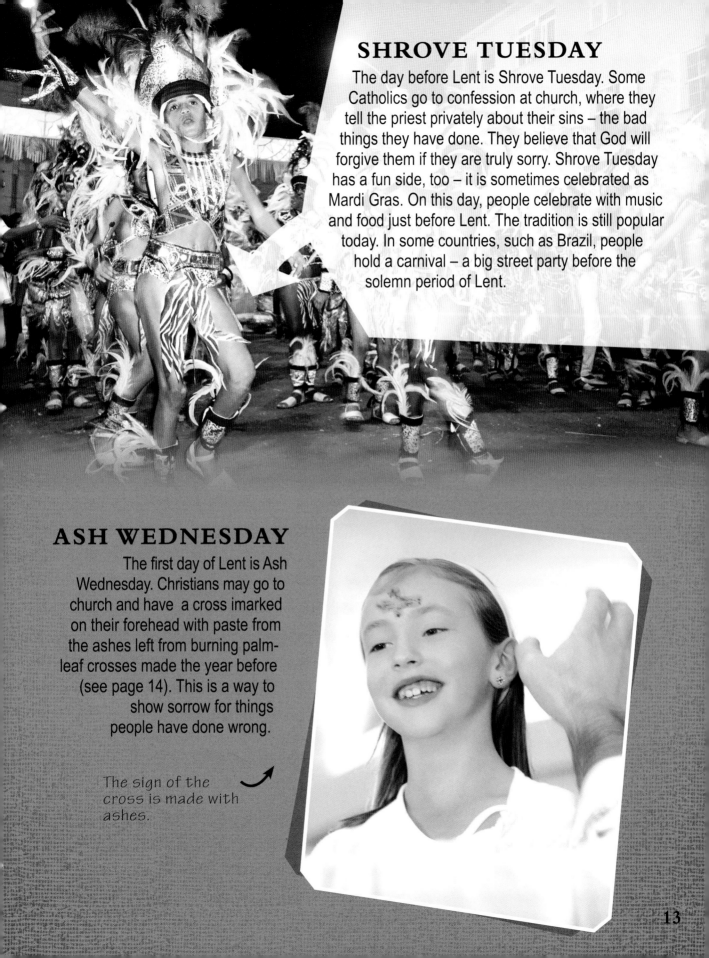

SHROVE TUESDAY

The day before Lent is Shrove Tuesday. Some Catholics go to confession at church, where they tell the priest privately about their sins – the bad things they have done. They believe that God will forgive them if they are truly sorry. Shrove Tuesday has a fun side, too – it is sometimes celebrated as Mardi Gras. On this day, people celebrate with music and food just before Lent. The tradition is still popular today. In some countries, such as Brazil, people hold a carnival – a big street party before the solemn period of Lent.

ASH WEDNESDAY

The first day of Lent is Ash Wednesday. Christians may go to church and have a cross imarked on their forehead with paste from the ashes left from burning palm-leaf crosses made the year before (see page 14). This is a way to show sorrow for things people have done wrong.

The sign of the cross is made with ashes.

13

HOLY WEEK

The last week of Lent is Holy Week, the most important time in the Christian calendar. Christians remember the last week of Jesus's life.

A palm cross is made by folding strips of leaves from a palm tree.

PALM SUNDAY

On Palm Sunday, people recall how Jesus rode into Jerusalem on a donkey, welcomed by crowds of people waving palm branches. Today, many churches hold processions to reenact the tale, with worshippers carrying crosses made from palm leaves.

HOLY THURSDAY

Holy Thursday is the day of Jesus's Last Supper with his disciples (followers). As part of the meal, he shared bread and wine with them, saying "this is my body" and "this is my blood." The story lives on through the Eucharist or Holy Communion ceremony (see page 9). On the evening of Holy Thursday, Jesus told his followers that one of them would betray him. Indeed, his disciple Judas did betray him to the Roman rulers.

FOOT WASHING

On Holy Thursday, Jesus washed his followers' feet to show humbleness, as it was a job normally done by servants. Today, the Pope (the head of the Catholic Church) repeats the ritual.

GOOD FRIDAY AND HOLY SATURDAY

Good Friday is the most solemn day of Holy Week, when people remember Jesus's death. Jesus carried his heavy cross to the hill where he would be crucified. In the morning, some Christians march holding wooden crosses and may fast to help them focus on their prayers. Another custom in some countries is to eat hot cross buns. They have a serious purpose – to remind people that Jesus died on the cross.

Holy Saturday is the final day. At Orthodox churches, people begin a vigil at midnight on Easter Saturday and act out the story of the Resurrection – Jesus rising from the dead (see page 16).

This 17th-century crucifixion statue shows Jesus's death on the cross.

THE JOY OF EASTER

According to the Bible, after dying on the cross on Friday, Jesus returned to life once more on Sunday. To Christians, his resurrection was a miraculous "act of God" and the most significant event in their history. They believe that through their faith in Jesus's resurrection, they will be forgiven for their sins and saved. After death they will be with God in heaven.

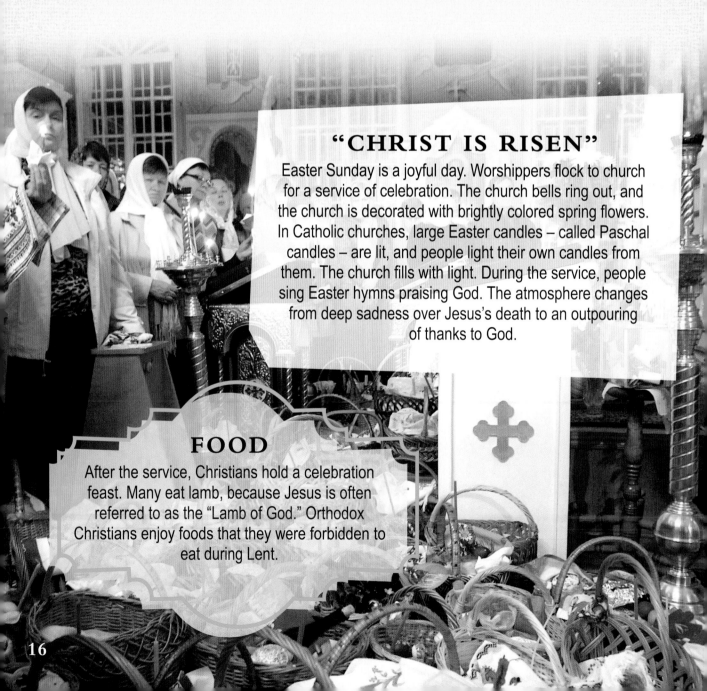

"CHRIST IS RISEN"

Easter Sunday is a joyful day. Worshippers flock to church for a service of celebration. The church bells ring out, and the church is decorated with brightly colored spring flowers. In Catholic churches, large Easter candles – called Paschal candles – are lit, and people light their own candles from them. The church fills with light. During the service, people sing Easter hymns praising God. The atmosphere changes from deep sadness over Jesus's death to an outpouring of thanks to God.

FOOD

After the service, Christians hold a celebration feast. Many eat lamb, because Jesus is often referred to as the "Lamb of God." Orthodox Christians enjoy foods that they were forbidden to eat during Lent.

EGGS AND BUNNIES

Children may make Easter eggs, painting hard-boiled eggs in bright colors. They go on Easter egg hunts, searching for chocolate eggs. There are special Easter foods, too. In parts of Europe, people eat simnel cake, a deliciously rich fruit cake, decorated with 11 marzipan balls to stand for all the disciples – except Judas, the disciple who betrayed Jesus (see page 14).

In parts of Europe and North America, the story of the Easter Bunny is popular. The bunny lays and hides eggs for children to find. Of course, rabbits don't really lay eggs. They do, however, have lots of babies, so like eggs, rabbits are a symbol of new life.

EASTER EGGS

Eggs are associated with new life because birds and many other animals hatch from eggs. The idea of new life can also mean life after death. Christians believe that when people pass away, they begin a new life with God.

17

HARVEST FESTIVAL

In some places, taking part in a harvest festival is part of growing up Christian. At this cheerful event in autumn, people celebrate the newly gathered crops, fruit, and vegetables. For Christians, God plays a vital role in nature.

GOD'S GIFTS

At a harvest service, the church is decorated with flowers, and people bring fresh produce for blessing. They sing hymns praising God for sending rain and sunshine to allow the crops to grow and provide food from the earth. Christians believe that all good gifts come from God.

Harvest is a time for sharing. Many churches collect food and basic goods to give to needy people in the community. Children often visit elderly people to bring them these gifts. Christians also send money to charities working to support people in poverty at home and abroad.

SHARING WITH OTHERS

"We all have so much more than we need. We have not just daily bread but freezers full. So we must learn gratitude and sharing. No matter how poor we may seem, we all have some gift or contribution we can make for the betterment of all."
- The Reverend Charles Royden

HARVEST FUN

Around the world, people celebrate the harvest. In Germany, *Erntedankfest* (harvest festival) takes place on the first Sunday in October. At church, people make donations to charity. Then there's a parade around town. Dancers dressed in traditional folk costumes and musicians take part, and hundreds gather to watch the music and dancing. A traditional harvest crown is presented to the harvest queen. Sometimes there's an evening service, too, and a lantern parade for children.

For many Christians in the United States, Thanksgiving is a day to thank God for the harvest throughout the year. Many attend church before enjoying a spectacular feast with friends and family gathered from far and wide.

GROWING UP CHRISTIAN

Worship is not just for festivals. From an early age, Christians bring their faith into their daily life. Before meals, many families say grace – a prayer to thank God for providing food. People pray alone, too – at bedtime, for example. They praise God's greatness, say they're sorry for doing wrong, or ask for help. Prayer is all about connecting with God and trying to be a better person.

AN IRISH GRACE

"Bless, O Lord, this food we are about to eat; and we pray You, O God, that it may be good for our body and soul; and if there be any poor creature hungry or thirsty walking along the road, send them in to us that we can share the food with them, just as You share your gifts with all of us."

COMMUNION AND CONFIRMATION

Rites of passage mark the stages of growing up as a Christian. Catholic children take their First Holy Communion when they are about seven years old.

In many churches, including Anglican, Protestant, Orthodox, and Catholic churches, children confirm their faiths when they are around 13 to 16 years old. This is thought to be old enough to understand what it means to be a Christian. They restate the promises made for them when they were baptized. Catholics, Anglicans, and some other church branches hold a confirmation service. Groups of children attend classes to prepare for this important occasion.

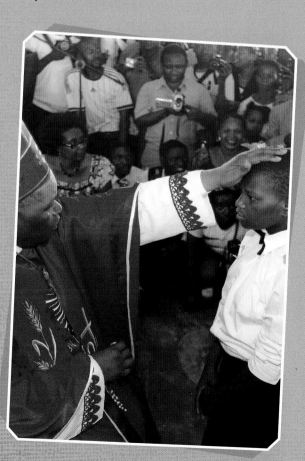

JOINING THE CHRISTIAN FAMILY

On confirmation day, many children are nervous but excited. The bishop conducts the service. In front of the whole congregation, he asks them questions one by one to check that they understand their religion. One question is "Do you believe and trust in God the Father, who made the world?"

Afterwards, the children kneel at the altar rail, and the bishop places his hands on each of their heads in turn. Catholic and Anglican priests anoint the children's foreheads with a little oil, a symbol of strength and the power to resist evil. The young people are now full members of the Christian family.

CHRISTIANS IN THE COMMUNITY

Christians don't only share with others at festivals. A central part of being a Christian is to help others in the community all year round – whether they are Christians, people of other faiths, or follow no religion.

HELPING HANDS

One of the duties of priests and ministers is to help those in need. They visit elderly people living alone, especially if they are ill. Ministers offer a listening ear if people need to talk about their troubles. They may organize meals and advice for homeless people. In freezing winter weather, they might arrange for volunteers to bring much-needed food supplies to people who cannot leave the house safely to go shopping.

COMMUNITY

Churches host youth clubs offering all kinds of entertainment, from games and film nights to sports and music. Church halls are frequently home to a variety of community activities for people of all ages, such as parent and toddler groups, yoga, singing groups, and fitness classes.

A HEART FOR SERVICE

"St. Luke's is a parish church that aims to serve everyone in the area, whether they come to church or not. We open the church three days a week for volunteers to serve hot meals on a 'pay as you feel' basis and have a monthly drop-in for the homeless. We run groups for toddlers and teenagers and provide spiritual care for anyone who asks."
(Martin Poole, St. Luke's Church, Brighton, UK)

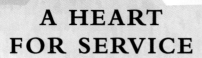

CHARITY COLLECTIONS

Church congregations also partner with organizations that work in poor communities around the world and help to raise money for charities. For example, every year, the charity Christian Aid organizes Christian Aid Week. People collect money at church, go around collecting from houses, and host fundraising breakfasts. Participating in community work is all part of being a good Christian and a member of the one big family of Christianity.

WEDDING CELEBRATIONS

Within the wider family of the church, Christians often want to have families of their own. Getting married and having children is mentioned in the Bible many times, and it can be an important part of Christian life. When a person meets someone special, the pair become engaged, and most Christians decide to marry at church.

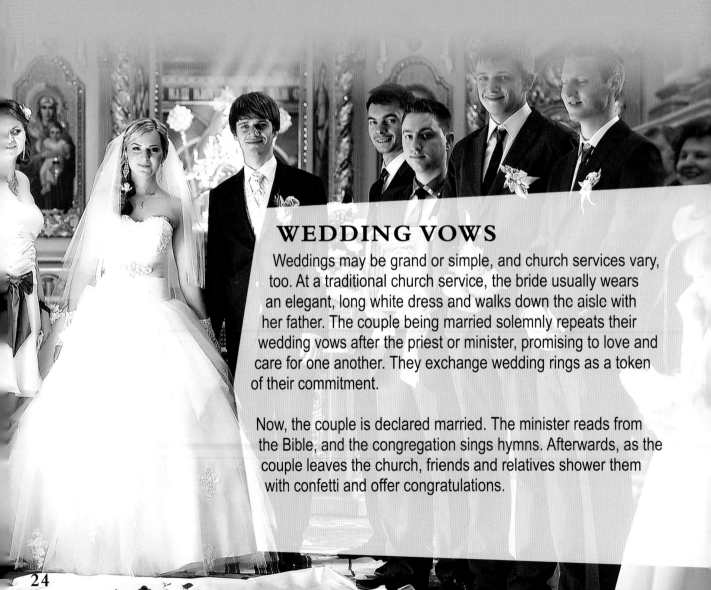

WEDDING VOWS

Weddings may be grand or simple, and church services vary, too. At a traditional church service, the bride usually wears an elegant, long white dress and walks down the aisle with her father. The couple being married solemnly repeats their wedding vows after the priest or minister, promising to love and care for one another. They exchange wedding rings as a token of their commitment.

Now, the couple is declared married. The minister reads from the Bible, and the congregation sings hymns. Afterwards, as the couple leaves the church, friends and relatives shower them with confetti and offer congratulations.

PARTY!

After the service comes the reception. Traditionally, important people in the couple's lives may make speeches and wish the couple happiness. Often, the pair feed each other slices of wedding cake, to symbolize how they will look after each other. The party includes music and dancing. Soon afterwards, the couple may go on their honeymoon, a special vacation to start married life.

SAME-SEX MARRIAGE

Worldwide, the church is divided over same-sex marriage. Some branches accept the marriage of LGBTQI people and feel they should have the same rights as others. Other branches are against such relationships.

WHEN MARRIAGE GOES WRONG

The Bible teaches that marriage is for life and generally does not approve of people marrying again after a divorce. But sometimes marriages fail. Christians do not encourage divorce, but some branches of Christianity believe that they should show forgiveness to divorced people and allow them to marry again in church. Others do not permit divorced people to remarry in church, but may allow a blessing service instead.

PILGRIMAGES

A pilgrimage is a journey to a place that is holy to your religion, often at the time of a festival. Some pilgrims travel alone, while others go with a group. A pilgrimage is a unique experience, and some Christians save up for years to go.

Pilgrims often visit St. Peter's Basilica, a huge Catholic church in Vatican City, Italy.

A REAL JOURNEY

Going on a pilgrimage helps people to strengthen their religious beliefs and feel closer to God. As well as being a real-life journey, it can be an inner journey, helping people to understand themselves. Pilgrims thank God for the good things in life, seek his forgiveness for committing bad deeds, and might ask for his help.

SIGNIFICANT SITES

There are Christian pilgrimage sites around the world. Catholics often head to Vatican City in Rome, Italy, to listen to the Pope's teachings. Many Christians visit the Holy Land to visit places that were significant in Jesus's life. They enter the beautiful Church of the Nativity, which marks his birthplace in Bethlehem. They travel to Nazareth, where Jesus lived as a boy, and visit sites in Galilee and Capernaum, where it is said that miracles occurred.

LOURDES

Many Christians believe that Jesus's mother, known as the Virgin Mary, appeared to a young girl in Lourdes, France, in 1858. She told the girl where to find healing water. To this day, pilgrims go to Lourdes if they are ill to fetch holy water or for healing ceremonies.

EASTER PROCESSION

At Easter, pilgrims join the procession in the holy city of Jerusalem. Thousands of people walk slowly through the Via Dolorosa (Way of Sorrow), carrying wooden crosses, praying, and singing hymns. They trace Jesus's last steps toward his death on the cross. It is particularly moving to reenact the events at the site where they took place 2,000 years ago.

LIFE'S END

For Christians, the journey through life can be seen as a pilgrimage. At its end, faith is a great comfort. Christians who know they are dying may make their peace with people they have argued with. If possible, in their final hours, a priest or minister prays with them at their bedside. Roman Catholics have the Last Rites, during which a priest anoints them with holy oil.

FUNERAL SERVICE

Once the person has died, the body is washed, dressed, and placed in a coffin. A hearse takes the coffin to church for the funeral service. Members of the congregation wear dark clothes to show respect and may send wreaths of flowers or give money to their loved one's favorite charity. A priest or minister leads the service, saying a few words to comfort the mourners, followed by prayers and readings from the Bible. Relatives and friends may retell fond memories of the person who has died.

BURIAL OR CREMATION

Christians can choose to be buried or cremated. At a burial, the coffin is lowered into the ground in a cemetery or churchyard and covered with earth. Later a headstone will mark the grave. If the person is cremated, the ashes are returned to the family to bury in a cemetery or churchyard or to scatter in their relative's favorite place.

LIFE WITH GOD

Christians believe that death is not the end and that the soul of the person who has passed away will have a new life with God. Christians are sad because they will not see their loved one again in this life. Yet they believe that one day they will be reunited with everyone they have lost in heaven.

EVERLASTING LIFE

When the coffin is lowered or the curtains close around it for cremation, these words are said: "We therefore commit (his or her) body to the ground; earth to earth, ashes to ashes, dust to dust; in the sure and certain hope of the resurrection to eternal (everlasting) life."

The ashes of a loved one who has died are collected in a funeral urn.

Undertakers carefully lower the coffin into the grave.

GLOSSARY

anoint To put a little oil on someone's head as part of a religious ceremony

baptism A Christian ceremony in which a few drops of water are poured on a baby to welcome them into the Christian Church. Adults can also be baptized by being immersed in water

bishop The minister in charge of the churches in a large area called a diocese

cathedral The main church of a district, under the care of a bishop

Catholic A person who is a member of the Roman Catholic Church, the branch of the church that has the Pope as its leader

commandment A religious law, in particular one of the Ten Commandments in the Bible

confession In the Catholic branch of Christianity, a religious duty in which people tell a priest privately about things they have done wrong, saying they are sorry for wrongdoing and asking for God's forgiveness

congregation A group of people who are gathered together in a church to worship God, not including the priest and choir

cremate To burn a dead body as part of a funeral ceremony

crucifixion Killing somebody by fastening them to a wooden cross and leaving them there to die

disciples Jesus's twelve followers

Eucharist A church service in which people eat a little bread and drink some wine to remember Jesus. The bread stands for his body and the wine stands for his blood.

gospel choir A choir that sings Christian religious music in a blues style that was created by African Americans

hearse A long, black funeral car for carrying coffins

Holy Communion Another name for the Eucharist ceremony

Holy Land The area of the biblical land of Israel and the historical country of Palestine

Holy Spirit The third part of God in the Trinity, along with God and Jesus. The Holy Spirit is the power of God in the world.

hymn A song that Christians sing to praise God

lectern The stand from which the Bible is read during a church service

LGBTQI Stands for lesbian, gay, bisexual, transexual, queer, and intersex

modestly Dress in a way that does not show much of the body

nativity scene A model of the baby Jesus and his family in the stable where he was born

Orthodox Church The branch of the church that separated from the Catholic Church about 1,000 years ago. It includes the Russian and Greek churches.

pilgrimage A journey to a holy place

preach To give a religious talk in church or another public place

prophecy A statement that something will happen in the future; in Christianity, it is someone who can receive a message from God

Protestant Church The part of the Western Christian Church that separated from the Roman Catholic Church in the 16th century

pulpit The stand where the priest or minister stands to give the sermon – a talk on a religious subject

soul The spiritual part of a person, which Christians believe exists after death

Vatican The group of buildings in Rome where the Pope lives and works inside Vatican City, a city-state within Rome

vigil The period of time when a group of people stay awake at night, often for a religious reason such as saying prayers

FIND OUT MORE

Books

Bodden, Valerie. *Understanding Christianity*. Minneapolis, MN: Abdo Publishing, 2018.

Ganeri, Anita. *Celebrating Weddings Around the World*. Chicago, IL: Heinemann Raintree, 2016.

Steinberg, Lynnae D. *Christianity*. New York, NY: Britannica Educational Publishing, 2019.

Websites
Christianity - An Introduction
www.bbc.co.uk/schools/religion/christianity/
Find out more about Christianity on this page.

Christmas
www.dkfindout.com/us/more-find-out/festivals-and-holidays/christmas
This page offers an overview of Christmas.

The Spread of Christianity
kidspast.com/world-history/christianity/
This page has information on some of the history surrounding Christianity.

INDEX